AF364970

Author: Syeda Atika Yahya

Illustrated by: Anisa Istiani Solichah

© 2026 Syeda Atika Yahya
All rights reserved. No part of this publication may be reproduced, stored in a retrieval system, or transmitted in any form or by any means electronic, mechanical, photocopying, recording, or otherwise without the prior written permission of the publisher, except for brief quotations used in reviews or critical articles.

ISBN: 978-93-342-1515-1
Published by Habeeb Book House
Hyderabad, India – 500008
First Indian Edition, 2026
Printed in India on eco-friendly paper

Illustrations ©Anisa Solichah
Instagram: @anisasolichah

For more inspiring writings, visit: www.atikayahya.com
Follow on Instagram: @syeda_atika_yahya

Dedication and Acknowledgements

To my children, who remind me every single day of the questions and courage that live inside little hearts. You inspired this book not just by your presence, but by your struggles, your wonderings, and your faith. This is for you.

Heartfelt thanks to my parents who still have my back, always with their quiet duas and unwavering belief in me, to my siblings, whose loyalty lit my path. And to my dearest husband–my anchor and my cheerleader. Your constant faith in me made all the difference.

Deepest gratitude to Sister **Naima B. Robert**, whose wisdom, encouragement, and unwavering support breathed life into this book and into my own voice as a writer. To my Writers' Hub community, your cheers, nudges, and belief in me carried me through to believing in myself as a writer.

Allah loves you, even if you do something wrong.
When Adam (عليه السلام) made a mistake,

Allah taught him to repent and return to him;
He Forgave him.

Allah cares for you, and He is Al-Ghafur, the one who always forgives.

Allah loves you,
even if people make fun of you and mock you.

When Noah (عليه السلام) built a boat,
the people made fun of him,
but they soon found out how wrong they were.

Allah knows your sincerity.
He is Al-Aleem, the All-Knowing.

Allah loves you,
even when you have lost someone special,
and you grieve for them.
When Yaqub (عليه السلام) grieved the loss of his son,
he cried his heart out, but he never lost hope or trust in Allah.

He held on to patience for years until his son was returned to him.

Allah knows your pain.
He is Al-Shaafi, the Healer.

Allah loves you,
even if everyone around doesn't trust you
and calls you a liar.

When no one trusted Yusuf (عليه السلام) and
they had him put in prison.

He remained patient, and eventually,
they trusted him with all the treasures of the land.

Allah knows your honesty. He is Al-Haqq,
the absolute truth.

Allah loves you,
even if you feel afraid,
and that fear grips you all around.

When the mother of Musa (عليه السلام) was scared
that Pharaoh might kill her child,

She remained hopeful,
and Allah brought her son back to her.
Allah knows your fear. He is Al-Haadi, the Guide.

Allah loves you,
even if you feel trapped and can't find a
solution to a problem.

When Musa (عليه السلام) was stuck
between the sea and the Pharaoh's Army,

He believed that Allah would make a way for him, and
Allah paved a path through the middle of
the sea.
Allah knows your faith.

He will provide you with solutions
you never imagined.
He is Al-Qadir, the capable and the powerful.

When Younus (عليه السلام) became tired of his people's behavior and gave up on them,

Allah inspired him to make a heartfelt prayer,

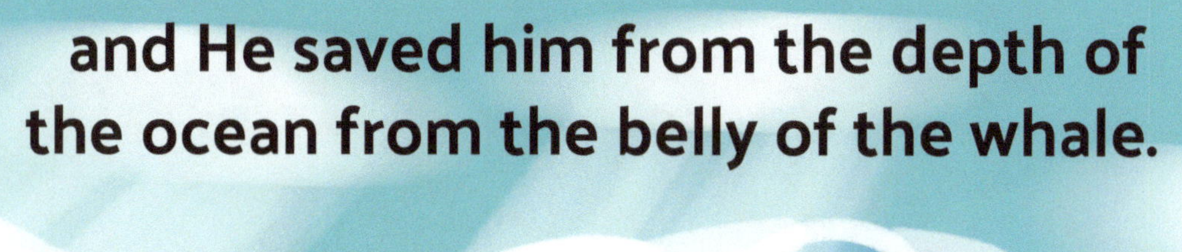

and He saved him from the depth of
the ocean from the belly of the whale.

Allah knows your forbearance.
He is Al-Haleem, the most forbearing.

Allah loves you, even if
you are afflicted with hardships.

When Ayyub (عليه السلام) was afflicted
with the loss of health, wealth, and even his family,
he never lost hope.

And Allah returned to him blessings better than he had before.

Allah knows your pure heart.
He is Al-Jabbar, the compeller.

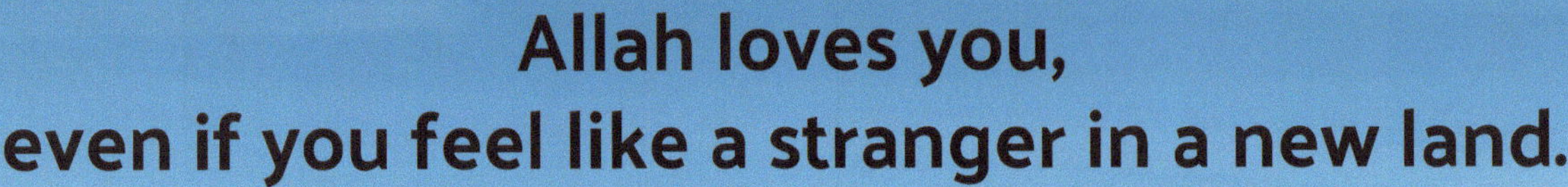

Allah loves you,
even if you feel like a stranger in a new land.

When Muhammed ﷺ left Mecca for Medina, he missed his hometown.

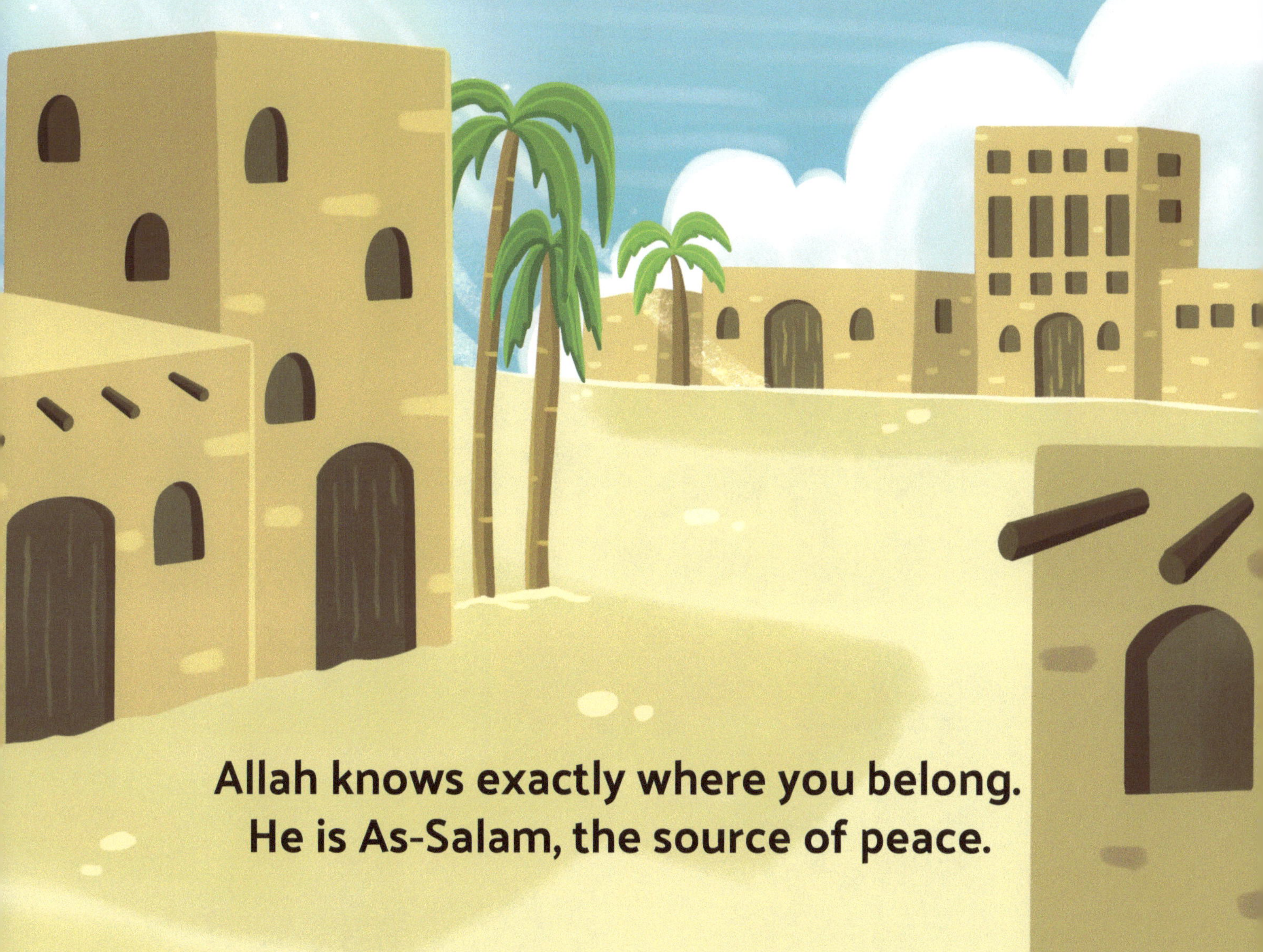

But he came to love his new home because the people of Madina helped him in every way they could.

Allah knows exactly where you belong.
He is As-Salam, the source of peace.

Allah loves you more than you can ever imagine.
He loves you 70 times more than Mama and Baba loves
you.

And when you feel that love, you will realize what amazing power you possess.

Dua of Adam (عليه السلام)
When you make a mistake, say the dua
Adam (عليه السلام) made to Allah.
He admitted his mistake and asked Allah for forgiveness.
Allah loves when we say sorry and turn back to Him.

رَبَّنَا ظَلَمْنَا اَنْفُسَنَا وَاِنْ لَّمْ تَغْفِرْ لَنَا وَتَرْحَمْنَا لَنَكُوْنَنَّ مِنَ الْخٰسِرِيْنَ

Rabbanaa zalamnaa anfusanaa wa illam taghfir lanaa wa

tarḥamnā lanakoonanna minal khaasireen

"Our Lord, we have wronged ourselves, and if You do not

forgive us and have mercy upon us, we will surely be among
the losers."
(Surah Al-A'raf: 23)

Dua of Yunus (عليه السلام)

When Prophet Yunus (عليه السلام) was trapped inside the belly of the whale, he made a very powerful dua. He admitted his mistake and praised Allah.

لَّا اِلٰهَ اِلَّاۤ اَنْتَ سُبْحٰنَكَ اِنِّيْ كُنْتُ مِنَ الظّٰلِمِيْنَ

Laa ilaaha illaa Anta, Subhaanaka innee kuntu minaz-zaalimeen

"There is no deity except You; glory be to You! Indeed, I was of the wrongdoers."
(Surah Al-Anbiya: 87)

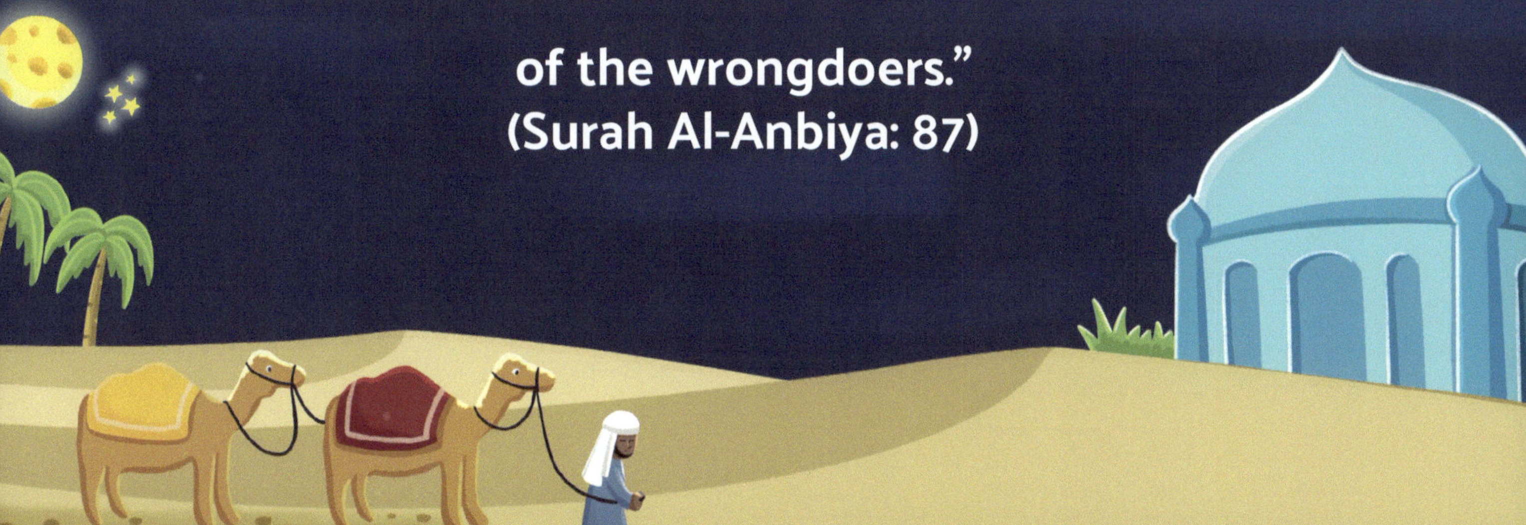

Dua of Nuh (عليه السلام)
When Nuh (عليه السلام) was mocked and felt helpless, he asked Allah for help.

رَبَّهٗٓ اَنِّيْ مَغْلُوْبٌ فَانْتَصِرْ

Rabbi innee maghloobun fantasir

"My Lord, I am overpowered, so help me!"
(Surah Al-Qamar: 10)

Dua of Ayyub (عليه السلام)

When Ayyub (عليه السلام) was very sick and in pain, he made this dua.
He didn't complain—he just asked gently for Allah's mercy

اِنِّي مَسَّنِيَ الضُّرُّ وَاَنْتَ اَرْحَمُ الرّٰحِمِينَ

Annee massaniya ad-durru wa Anta arhamur-raahimeen

"Indeed, hardship has touched me, and You

are the Most Merciful of the merciful."
(Surah Al-Anbiya: 83)

Dua of Musa (عليه السلام **)**
When Musa (عليه السلام) felt nervous to speak to Pharaoh,
he made this dua.
It gave him courage and confidence.

رَبِّ اشْرَحْ لِي صَدْرِي ۙ وَيَسِّرْ لِي أَمْرِي ۙ وَاحْلُلْ عُقْدَةً مِّن لِّسَانِي
يَفْقَهُوا قَوْلِي

Rabbish-rah lee sadree • Wa yassir lee amree • Wahlul

'uqdatan min lisanee • Yafqahoo qawlee

"My Lord, expand my chest with comfort,
make my task easy, and untie the
knot from my tongue so they
may understand my speech."
(Surah Taha: 25-28)

www.ingramcontent.com/pod-product-compliance
Lightning Source LLC
LaVergne TN
LVHW071702180726
843512LV00002B/525